Wha

This is a powerful, practical book full of proven — *help you get more done in less time and balance your life.*

– Brian Tracy,
President, Brian Tracy International

Busy Being Busy *is a simply amazing book! Simple because it is so true and easy to implement. Amazing because when you do your productivity, your happiness, and your free time goes way up!*

– Tom Ziglar,
CEO Ziglar, Proud Son of Zig Ziglar

If you're ready to get more done in less time and live a life of freedom, then read and use the strategies in this brilliant book by my friend, Michelle Prince!

– James Malinchak,
Featured on ABC's Hit TV Show, "Secret Millionaire"
Founder, www.BigMoneySpeaker.com

Are you're looking for practical solutions to getting more done in less time? I mean, real life examples not just a bunch of theory or complicated systems to follow? Then look no further! I might know a little bit about this topic… having written 5 best-selling books myself while running an international company at the same time. If I found this book useful doing all that I do, you will too.

– Loral Langemeier,
New York Times Bestselling Author,
www.liveoutloud.com

One of the biggest challenges small business owners face is staying organized, focused and productive in the face of overwhelming demands on their time. Michelle has done a phenomenal job sharing how to live a more balanced life in this book!

– Howard Partridge,
Best-Selling Author, Business Coach
and President of Phenomenal Products, Inc.

Michelle Prince has hit a home run with her book, Busy Being Busy! *We can all relate to being so busy that we sometimes lose sight of the big picture and what's really important in life. Michelle's easy-going style will encourage you to stop being busy and start living the life you always wanted!*

– Vicki Irvin,
CEO, Superwoman Lifestyle,
www.SuperwomanLifestyle.com

Michelle Prince's book, 'Busy Being Busy' is truly inspiring. This book will help you prioritize your life and only be "busy" doing the things that really matter. Michelle does it again with another highly recommended book!

– Natasha Duswalt,
Owner, Peak Models & Talent, Los Angeles, CA,
www.PeakModels.com

If you want a blueprint for getting more done in life, then you need to read Michelle Prince's book, 'Busy Being Busy.' You already have the tools you need, and Michelle shows you how to use them. Bottom line — this book ROCKS!

– Craig Duswalt,
Speaker, Author, Radio Host and Creator of the
RockStar System for Success, www.CraigDuswalt.com

Busy Being Busy *is the book to stop the cycle of a life that doesn't fulfill you. Read it now to have the life you want. Michelle Prince will show you how!*

– Jill Lublin,
International Speaker & Best-Selling Author of 3 Books,
Including Guerrilla Publicity.

Visit PublicityCrashCourse.com for free book

Busy Being Busy *is a quick and powerful read. This is THE essential guide to being more productive, accomplishing more and experiencing greater success!*

– Scott Schilling,
Best-Selling Author, Speaker / Trainer,
ScottSchilling.com

Michelle's latest book, "Busy Being Busy...But Getting Nothing Done," is the answer for anyone who struggles with too much to do and too little to show for it except more stress and frustration. Written as a step-by-step blueprint. She makes the transformation extremely easy to understand and apply. Say goodbye to procrastination and hello to a balanced life and the ability to attain the goals you never thought possible! Highly recommended!

– David Phelps, D.D.S.,
www.DiscoverFreedomHere.com

Who better to teach you how to get your life under control than a woman who actually did it! A mother, a speaker, seminar leader, coach and mentor who actually took herself from the state of chaos and uncertainty to one of simplicity and control to become one of the exemplars of eliminating procrastination and having a life that is balanced, under control and worth living.

– Mark Ehrlich,
The Coach to the Coaches, Founder,
CXO Partners, Inc

As the world's fastest reader, and author of dozens of programs, I know a lot about getting more done in less time. That's why I love Michelle's down-to-earth approach to getting things done in a fraction of the time with much better results. Her book, "Busy Being Busy," should be put at the top of your reading list. It is full of valuable information that you are going to love. This book will change your life.

– Howard Stephen Berg,
The World's Fastest Reader

Michelle Prince is a real Champion! I've had the honor of knowing her for several years and have seen her tremendous impact on others. Michelle has a sincere desire to change lives and make a real difference in the world. I'm confident that she will succeed!

– John Di Lemme,
International Motivational Speaker
& Strategic Business Coach

Michelle's book came at just the right time in my life. I was going through a difficult time in my personal life at the same time I was re-launching my business—there was a lot going on and all the goals I wanted to achieve were overshadowed by all the tasks and projects I thought I had to do in order to achieve my goals. To say that I was overwhelmed is an understatement. As a consequence I spent a lot of hours working, but not really accomplishing anything. Her book helped me take a step back and ask some simple yet powerful questions so that I could focus on what was important and take the right steps. Now I am glad to say that at the end of the day I have a greater sense of satisfaction about what I am accomplishing and I'm also noticing I have more time to be with family and friends without worrying about what should be getting done. Thanks Michelle.

– Kathryn Perry,
Transpersonal Coach & Entrepreneur

Fabulous truth telling from Michelle Prince about what no one wants to admit! This book is a must read for anyone who struggles with the overwhelm of life, which is ALL of us! Thank you Michelle for helpful strategies and real examples that we can put into use NOW.

– Diane Cunningham,
Founder and President, National Association
of Christian Women Entrepreneurs
www.nacwe.org

Michelle Prince has done it again! This book contains the most effective and practical blueprint for replacing being busy with being productive and enjoying yourself in the process. She has not only shared how to effectively manage our personal and business lives, but also reveals the pitfalls, traps and habits that can cause us to get out of balance. "Busy Being Busy" is a must read for anyone who wants to enjoy their life and their success.

– Nancy Matthews,
Speaker, Author & Success Catalyst
www.NancyMatthews.com

You can flip this book open to any page and find something meaningful that you can use right away. This isn't 'theory'—it's full of practical tips and tools you can put to use in your life immediately. Great information! Thanks, Michelle.

– Diane Lampe,
President, The Lampe Company, LLC,
Best-Selling Author

Michelle's book is a rare gem among the thousands of books on productivity. She gives you actionable steps to stop being busy and find your balance, so you can ultimately save yourself time, heartache and missing out on the life of your dreams. I suggest you grab a cup of coffee, a pen and her book, and then sit down to turn your life from one of chaos and overwhelm to one of productivity and ease. Thank you, Michelle, for putting together a blueprint for a balanced life!

– Kim Hodous, The Kitchen Table CEO
and Best-Selling Author of *Show Up, Be Bold, Play Big:*
33 Strategies for Outrageous Success and Lasting Happiness from a Former Stay-at-Home Mom who Built a
7-Figure Business from her Kitchen Table

Time is the only key area in our lives that we can't produce more of no matter how hard we work, and the one thing we never have enough of. Michelle Prince's book, *Busy Being Busy*, is a much needed resource that will empower us to create a more balanced and prosperous life. She teaches us how to define and stay focused on our priorities as well as how to create a plan to stop wasting time and move forward in a more purposeful and productive manner so we can live a happier and healthier life. I can't wait until my members have the chance to learn from this book.

– Christie Ruffino,
President and Founder of the
Dynamic Professional Women's Network

Michelle gets it! One of the most professional, organized people I know. This book is for EVERYONE; taking action and getting things done makes us all feel like what we do matters! Thanks Michelle.

– Dr. Scott F. Peterson,
Dental Marketing Magic

Michelle has a practical, straight-forward approach to help you re-prioritize, re-organize and re-energize. This 'how to' book is a call to action for anyone who needs to go from being busy to being productive. A must read!

– Debbie Hague

Michelle's practical step by step process of managing busyness is right on target! Tapping into her wisdom in life coach training for personal development was the best investment I have ever made towards business growth and expansion!

– Terri Lynn Schmidt

Busy Being Busy . . . But Getting Nothing Done?

THE ULTIMATE GUIDE

TO STOP JUGGLING,
OVERCOM PROCRASTINATION,
AND GET MORE DONE IN LESS TIME
IN BUSINESS, LEADERSHIP & LIFE

MICHELLE PRINCE

DEDICATION

This book is dedicated to those who know their life has more meaning than just a "To-Do" list; who want to live with passion, follow their purpose and make an impact in this world; to those who are ready to stop being busy *being* busy and are ready to start living a more joyful, meaningful life!

Contents

Introduction

*A*re you busy *being* busy?

Do you find that the details of your daily life take up so much of your time that you never seem to accomplish anything?

I know exactly how you feel!

A few years ago, I was busy managing a demanding job that required long hours in the office and many days on the road; I was raising two young boys; and I was trying to be a terrific wife, friend, daughter, employee, etc. I juggled exercise, kids' events, church, work, family commitments, date nights with my husband, parties, etc.

Good friends would watch me running around like a crazy woman and say, "How do you do it?"

"NOT VERY WELL!" I would respond.

The truth was, I got to be an expert juggler. I could keep all of those balls up in the air for a long time. But I eventually learned that there were better ways to manage the insanity of my life, and that is what this book

> *All the significant breakthroughs were breaks with old ways of thinking.*
>
> **—Thomas Kuhn**

is all about. Just a few adjustments to my routine gave me the balance I so desperately needed, and with that came a new peace and renewed energy to accomplish more than I had ever dreamed possible.

If you are busy *being* busy… but getting nothing done, you don't have to live that way any longer. Follow the tips in this book, and you will find yourself getting more done in less time. You have the power to make incredible changes in your business life and your personal life, and the time to start is right now.

Thank you for joining me on this exciting journey. Put down those juggling balls and walk with me…

Success to Me Is...

I want you to imagine for just one moment what it would be like if you could accomplish just your top two goals in your life. How different would your life look if you could do that?

Maybe one of your top goals is to make $5,000 more a month—or $10,000 more. You might have a goal of writing a book, or losing weight, or taking a trip to an exotic location in a country you've never been to before.

Look at your top two goals and really imagine yourself accomplishing them. How would that change your life? Can you see it? Paint a very vivid picture of what it will be like to achieve those two goals, because if you can hold on to that picture, you can make it happen.

Here's another question: What is your definition of success?

Sounds like a relatively harmless question, but it is a very important one, too. How do you define success? Fill in the rest of this sentence:

Success to me is...

_____

_____

_____

_____

_____

_____

_____

_____

_____

_____

_____

_____

_____

You know what? If I took a poll of everyone who read this book and asked them to finish that sentence, there would be as many different answers as people I interviewed. We all define personal success in completely different ways. None of us are exactly alike, and therefore we all have different dreams, desires, and images of how we would like our future to look.

Some people define success by fame, others look for prestige. One person may describe success as being able to build a business from nothing to one that makes millions of dollars. They define success, at least partially, in terms of money.

Another person may look to family relationships to define success. They will know they are successful if their family members are happy, healthy, and well cared for.

So when you get to the end of your life, and you are able to look back and say, "I was a success," what did you do? What did your life look like?

> *Visualizing something organizes one's ability to accomplish it.*
>
> **—Stephen R. Covey**

Take some time now to picture it, describe it, and write down your thoughts.

This is not just a silly exercise. It is crucial to your journey. If you don't know what success looks like, how will you recognize it when you get there? Or how will you know which direction to go to find it? You can't know you're a success if you are unable to define the term in the first place.

Jot down as many words or phrases as you can think of that define your idea of success. If you can articulate what it is you want, you will have a much greater chance of achieving it.

A Brief Detour

*N*ow, I'd like to take a little detour—well, actually, a very big detour. We're going back to the 1980s. That was a fun decade, wasn't it? If you aren't old enough to remember the '80s, then I'll give you a little glimpse into what I like to call "My Decade."

If you do remember the 1980s, take a moment to let your mind drift back to that crazy time. What images do you see?

Parachute pants?

Madonna?

Shoulder pads?

Big hair?

I jumped full force into the '80s. It was most definitely my time. I had the big hair, the shoulder pads, the hot-pink leg warmers. I came of age during these years, and so I embraced them, with all of their quirkiness.

Do you remember the Rubik's Cube?

That one baffled me. My brother solved it eventually, but I couldn't do it. Finally, I pulled off the stickers and placed them where I wanted them to end up. That's how I solved the Rubik's Cube.

Another thing that personifies the '80s to me is Ronald Reagan. He was president for a majority of the 1980s, and he was *my* president. I think of him when I think of that time in my life.

Ah, the '80s. It was a magical time.

So by now you must be thinking, *Why are we talking about the '80s? What in the world does this have to do with goal setting and procrastination? She's procrastinating in getting to the point, that's what's happening here!*

Trust me, there is a method to my madness.

I needed to set the stage. It is important for me to start in the '80s, because that is when an event occurred that changed my life forever. My entire life changed in 1989, and it changed in a way that I could have never predicted.

In 1989, I was just about to enter my first year of college at the University of North Texas in Denton, Texas. It was the week before classes started, and my mom came bounding into my room. She is an itty-bitty thing, and when she gets excited, she can literally bounce off the walls.

"Michelle, your dad and I have a big, big gift for you," she beamed, hopping up and down in place.

I thought, *It has got to be a car!*

What else could register this kind of excitement for a college-bound teen?

I was wrong. It was two tickets.

To a rock concert? To Disney World?

No.

Two tickets to a seminar.

At that brief moment, I lost almost all respect for my mother. I was eighteen years old. Come on, who wants to go to a seminar at that age?

And it gets worse.

It was a *motivational* seminar.

Were they trying to torture me?

I couldn't believe my terrible luck.

The worst part of all of this was the seminar was to take place the last weekend I had free before I would go off to college. Friends were everything to me at this point in my life. My friends and I were all about to take off to different colleges, and this was our last weekend together—our last big hurrah.

Were they kidding?

It had to be some sort of joke.

Well, I went to the seminar, and that weekend completely changed my life. I was surrounded by people who got it, who set goals, who wanted more out of life, who overcame procrastination, and who were successful. It was the best gift my parents could have ever given me. Turns out they're pretty brilliant, as parents go!

The seminar was called "Born to Win," and it was hosted by a guy named Zig Ziglar. At the time, I had no idea who he was. I didn't think I wanted to have anything to do with him at the beginning of the three-day seminar, but by the end, I was captivated. This one event truly set the foundation for everything I have become today.

At the end of the seminar, I couldn't wait to go shake Zig Ziglar's hand and get his autograph. This was the first time I had really heard about goal setting, building self-esteem, and how to have balance in your life—all things that we know are critical to success as an adult. It was new information to me that weekend, and I soaked it up like a sponge.

So I walked up to Zig Ziglar at the end of the seminar—and this is a true story. I felt compelled to tell Mr. Ziglar what a great job he did (as if he needed to hear it from me!).

I walked right up to him, shook his hand, and said, "Mr. Ziglar, thank you so much. You did a fabulous job. This has been the best weekend of my life. And by the way, I will work for you someday. You just wait and see. That's right, I will work for you one day."

And I meant it.

Meanwhile, my brother was standing next to me, wanting to crawl under a rock he was so embarrassed by what I had said.

But have you ever been in a situation where you just knew with every fiber of your being that some way, somehow, something was going to happen?

I knew that weekend that Zig Ziglar and his teaching would be a significant part of my life. I just knew it.

So what did I do?

I went off to college the following Monday morning and spent the next four-and-a-half years in school. When I emerged with a degree, ready to take on the world, the economy in the United States was about like it is right now, and I had a very hard time finding a job.

I swore I would never be a salesperson, but it looked like a sales position was my only option. I took a job selling copiers. Now, we are not talking little compact copiers. I sold those ginormous office copiers that had a zillion different buttons (or at least that's how it seemed). My job was to go around and demo them and hope that I could sell them to businesses. Not exactly my dream job.

I was cold calling in Carrollton, Texas, and back in those days, cold calling

> *Many people quit looking for work as soon as they find a job.*
>
> *—Zig Ziglar*

did not mean picking up the phone. It meant going from business to business, door to door, to try to talk to people about copiers.

I walked up to an office park there in Carrollton, and I looked up at the sign:

The Zig Ziglar Corporation

I about fell over! Zig Ziglar! I told this guy years ago I wanted to work for him. I wondered if he remembered me.

"That's right! I'm supposed to work here," I said

under my breath as I pulled open the big glass doors and walked into the building.

I was very lucky that the first person I ran into was the most wonderful, gracious woman in the world. Her name was Lou.

"My gosh! Is this really where Zig Ziglar works?" I gushed.

"Yes," she nodded.

"Do you have any job openings? I will do anything to work here!"

There was one job opportunity—Lou told me—in sales.

Sales?! Ugh.

It didn't matter. I would have cleaned toilets just to work for this man.

I dashed home and typed up my first resume—complete with my extensive job history selling copiers. By some miracle, I got a call from the VP of sales, and then an interview, and the rest is history. I got the job.

Now, I did not relay that story to impress you. Honestly, six months of selling copiers is not impressive, and it certainly isn't the hidden ingredient to getting a job working for Zig Ziglar.

I'm telling you this story, because the reason for my success was not my resume. It was my intention. I planted the seed when I was eighteen years old. I set a goal. I defined my idea of success.

I didn't worry about how I was going to get there or when I was going to get there. I simply planted the seed, and I was blessed to see that seed bear fruit and become my reality. I worked for the Zig Ziglar Corporation for about three years, and it was one of the best experiences of my entire life. It set me up to become what I have become today.

Now that you've heard part of my story, I have a question for you.

What's your story?

We all have a story. In fact, Zig will tell you that he believes every person has at least one book in them. So what's your story? What is the one thing that you have been through that has defined who you are today?

It doesn't necessarily have to be a happy story. We have all had good things and bad things that defined us or shaped our lives. Challenges are just as important as triumphs when it comes to your story.

Please take a moment to write down thoughts that come to mind when you answer this question. What is your story? It just might inspire someone else.

_____

_____

_____

_____

_____

_____

_____

_____

_____

_____

_____

_____

_____

———— WHICH WAY DO WE GO? ————

I told you a little bit of my story to get to a very important first tool for overcoming procrastination. Here it is:

Know Where You're Going

It's hard to reach success in any area if you don't have a goal in mind. People who actually accomplish their goals have a plan. It's pretty simple. They know where they're going.

It's easy to procrastinate when you're not really sure where you're going. You can wander around aimlessly for years. But if you know where you're going, you create a natu-

> *Character is the ability to carry out a good resolution long after the excitement of the moment has passed.*
>
> **—Cavett Robert**

ral sense of urgency. You want to get there as soon as possible and experience the happiness and fulfillment you deserve when you achieve that goal.

Think about anyone you know who is successful. They may be in your industry, in your community, or a relative or friend—someone you admire for the things they have achieved in their life. I guarantee you, if you asked them what they wanted to accomplish within the

> *The further you stray from your passion and purpose in life, the further you step away from true happiness.*
>
> **—Michelle Prince**

year, they would have a plan already in place. They already know where they're going, and they have the route all figured out. Decide where you're going, and you will have the opportunity to achieve very similar results.

Now, let me tell you a little bit more of my story. So there I was at age twenty-three, having reached a huge goal of working for Zig Ziglar. My dream came true, and every day of the three years I worked there, I was living my dream.

I can't tell you how amazing it was to know that I was making a difference in people's lives. Whether they bought a book, attended a seminar, or scheduled Zig to speak to their corporation, I knew that the content of the material would change their lives for the better. It was an incredible experience.

So what did I do at age twenty-three? I left.

It seems like a crazy idea, but the dotcom boom had just started, and I was lured away to the technology world to do software sales. For the first time in my life, I had to make a decision between two things: follow my passion or make more money.

The two options kept turning over and over in my mind. Follow my passion. Make more money. Follow my passion. Make more money. What do you think I chose? Yeah, I chose to make more money. And I did. I quit the Zig Ziglar Corporation, and although it was the hardest decision of my life, it's what needed to happen for me to be where I am today.

I spent the next twelve years in Corporate America. On the outside looking in, I appeared to be very successful. I had a great job. I was doing very well financially. I hit every one of my sales goals. On the outside I looked extremely successful and happy.

But that was so far from the truth. I can tell you that the further you stray from your passion and purpose in life, the further you step away from true happiness. I woke up, got my kids to daycare, went to work, paid the bills…I went through all the motions, but I was not in the least bit fulfilled. I was busy being busy, but I had no purpose behind my actions.

I started asking myself questions. Is this really all there is? Is this really my life? Is this it? And when I honestly answered those questions, I began to realize that success is not a number. It is not a dollar sign or an expensive car. It is about being fulfilled and living a life full of passion and purpose.

I eventually came to six very tough questions that I needed to answer in order to make a significant change in my life. I will share those questions with you now and encourage you to spend some time searching your soul and answering them for yourself. They will help you find your true purpose in life, as they helped me.

Question #1:

What activities do you enjoy?

_____

_____

_____

_____

_____

_____

_____

_____

_____

_____

This looks like a very simple question, but let me be a little more specific. This is not what do you love to do for work, or what do you love to do on the weekends. What do you really, really enjoy? When you are engaged in this activity, time flies by. Are you with your kids? Are you teaching? Maybe you are listening to someone who inspires you. Are you leading a group? Cooking? Creating? What activity captivates you so completely that you lose track of every-thing else around you?

By the way, don't try to think of only one answer to this question. Write down everything that comes to mind.

> *Don't compromise yourself. You are all you've got.*
>
> **—Betty Ford**

You can sift through your answers later and look for patterns or activities that stand out.

Question #2:

What would you do if you could not fail?

_____

_____

_____

_____

_____

_____

_____

_____

_____

_____

I had a really hard time answering this question when I was deep in Corporate America. I wasn't sure anymore what my purpose in life was, so I found it hard to think outside of the box that way. Spend some time with this question and let yourself dream big.

Let's take it one step further. If you could do anything in the world, money was no object (all of your bills were covered, your investments were handled, and you had no money worries), AND you had all the time in the world—and you couldn't fail—what would you do? It's interesting to ponder that question when the usual roadblocks are removed.

Would you be doing what you're doing today? Would you start a charity? Would you travel the world? Would you write a book? Write down anything that comes to mind.

I believe that your purpose in life is very closely tied to the things you enjoy, so this is not a frivolous exercise. Your answers are important to finding your purpose.

Question #3:

What ideas are you most inspired by?

_____

_____

_____

_____

_____

_____

_____

_____

There are a million possible answers to this question. You can be inspired in countless ways. Are you inspired by politics? Community concerns? The elderly?

If you're not sure where to start in answering this question, I'll give you another question: When you go to the bookstore, what section do you gravitate toward?

For me, it's always the personal development section. It makes perfect sense. That's my passion.

Where do you wander to when you walk into a bookstore? It might be the history section, or the cooking area. You can learn a lot about yourself by paying attention to where you end up in the bookstore.

> *You can learn a lot about yourself by paying attention to where you end up in the bookstore.*
> —**Michelle Prince**

Question #4:

When do you feel empowered?

_____

_____

_____

_____

_____

_____

_____

_____

_____

What I mean by *empowered* is when you feel like you're at your absolute best. Another related question that might get you closer to your answer is: What are you doing when people compliment you? What do others think you're good at doing?

Maybe you are a terrific manager, or an inspiring public speaker. You might be a good listener or an excellent teacher. When do you feel empowered? When are you at your best? Write down everything that comes to mind.

Question #5:

What is on your bucket list?

_____

_____

_____

_____

_____

_____

_____

_____

_____

_____

I'm sure you know all about the movie *The Bucket List*. It's about two old guys who are about to "kick the bucket," and they make a list of all the things they want to do before they die.

Do you have a bucket list?

If you don't, sit down right now and make one.

What do you keep saying you'll do someday? Put it on the list! Someday will get here sooner than you think.

There are absolutely no rules for this list. Write down anything that comes to mind—anything you want to do before you "kick the bucket."

Question #6:

What legacy do you want to leave?

_____

_____

_____

_____

_____

_____

_____

_____

_____

_____

_____

At the end of our lives, every single one of us is going to leave some kind of legacy. It's not just a legacy for your children. You will leave a legacy in your community, in your workplace, wherever you go. Your actions impact others. What sort of trail do you want to leave?

I love this last question, because it really allows you to back into your purpose in life. What is your legacy going to be? What do you want people to remember about you? Your accomplishments? Your character? If you think about the legacy you want to leave behind, you can work backward to discover what you need to do today to develop that legacy.

If you want to leave a lasting legacy, you can't wait until the last minute. Procrastination is not an option. What are you doing today to leave a legacy? Don't put it off. This is too important to leave to someday.

These six questions are so important. Once you know what you're passionate about, once you know what your purpose is, then you can set goals and really figure out what you want to do with your life, who you want to be, and what you want to have.

In order to really be productive in life you have to first *know where you're going.*

B.U.S.Y.

*B*USY...it's a four-letter word.

According to *Merriam-Webster*, the term busy means the following:

- Engaged in action.
- Full of activity.
- Foolishly or intrusively active.
- Full of distracting details.

Not all of those definitions are exactly positive, are they?

I would like to change your outlook on BUSY. It's time for this term to work for you, not against you. So I have come up with a new acronym for B.U.S.Y.:

Balance

Ultimately

Saves

You

The key really is balance. Those of us—and I do put myself in this category—who are very busy also have the tendency to put ourselves last. We take on the challenges of everyone around us. We are the go-to people.

"Take it to Michelle; she'll get it done."

Sound familiar?

The problem with this is that we often end up getting so busy that our lives become counterproductive. We deplete all of our resources and do not spend any time doing those things that fill us back up with energy, creativity, and joy. We lose balance.

So first, I would like to introduce you to a different circus act in my bag of tricks—not the juggling act. This is the balancing act, and I'll teach you how to become a pro.

Back in my juggling days, I really thought I had it all. I felt good when I was busy. To me, it was a much better alternative than being lazy. However, I realize now that constant juggling often spread me too thin. I have found that I am far more productive and happy when I strive to always maintain balance in

> *Insanity is the belief that you can keep on doing what you've been doing and get different results.*
>
> **—Albert Einstein**

my life. I eventually threw away my juggling balls, and now I work on my balancing act. The results have been wonderful.

Exercise is good; building a thriving business is good; spending time with family is good; church is good; nurturing relationships is good; studying is good—they're all good activities. But too much of any one thing is unhealthy, no matter how positive it looks on the outside.

It is very important to choose activities that recharge you and fill you up with exactly what you need to thrive. A balanced meal contains a variety of nutrients that serve different parts of the body and create a healthier overall you. You may choose to eat a balanced meal, and the result will be increased health and happiness. Or you may choose to eat junk food, filled with empty calories, and the result will be lethargy, weight gain, and potentially more serious health risks like diabetes.

It works the same when you balance your time. You will find out what activities fuel your lifestyle and also help you reduce stress. Those activities will become your priorities as you balance your way to a less crazy life.

Here's the good news: You get to choose!

Life is a series of choices. You are not a victim of fate. You choose the life you will lead.

Think of one choice you could make today that would improve your quality of life. Then, do it!

What about the opposite? Consider one thing that would make your life worse. Don't do that.

It's pretty simple when you get right down to it.
You may be thinking at this point, *Pretty simple, right! I'm so busy, I don't even know what is good for me and what isn't. I honestly don't have a clue what is taking up all my precious time every day.*

Let's find out what's going on in your life.

Exercise

In the following chart, you will see six core areas that cover the important general categories of your life. These areas include subcategories that will help you evaluate where you are in terms of personal satisfaction.

Rate your satisfaction in each area on a scale of 1 to 5:

5 is very satisfied—you feel like this area of your life is going well, and you have little need for improvement.

1 is unsatisfied—you are not happy with this area, and you have a lot of work to do here.

Please rate each area as honestly and accurately as you can. This will give you a picture of where you stand today, and it will point you in the direction of areas to target for improvement. The more honest you are in your self-evaluation, the faster you will move toward a more satisfying life.

Personal Growth	1	2	3	4	5
Hobbies					
Reading/Growth					
Education					
Attitude					
Having Fun					
Career	1	2	3	4	5
Enjoy Work					
Capable					
Appreciated					
Coworker Relationships					
Ability to Advance					
Relationships	1	2	3	4	5
Friends/Family					
Ability to Love					
Accepting					
Good Listener					
Open Communication					
Sense of Togetherness					
Financial	1	2	3	4	5
Budgets					
Earnings					
Savings					
Investments					

Debt					
Physical	**1**	**2**	**3**	**4**	**5**
Exercise					
Health					
Weight					
Diet					
Stress					
Spiritual	**1**	**2**	**3**	**4**	**5**
Inner Peace					
Church					
Belief					
Faith					
Prayer					
Purpose					

Now, take those numbers and plot them along the lines below, and play connect-the-dots by drawing a line from one number to the next.

PG	C	R	F	P	S
5	5	5	5	5	5
4	4	4	4	4	4
3	3	3	3	3	3
2	2	2	2	2	2
1	1	1	1	1	1

How does it look? Do you have a nice straight "road" to a balanced life along the fives across the top of the chart? Or do you notice quite a few "potholes" dipping down to lower numbers?

This will give you a visual guide of the areas where you will do some repair work to restore balance in your life. And you can put on your hard hat and get to work right now. Write down one thing you can do in each area where you would like to remove a pothole.

For example, if you rated your personal life a two, what could you do to get that number closer to five?

Here are some ideas:

• Set aside 30 minutes to read today
• Listen to a motivational CD on the way to work
• Sign up to take a creative writing class

You do not need to completely demolish your current schedule and start over. Just one or two changes a day in an area where you need work will bring you closer to a balanced life.

Immediate action is important, so in the space below, write down one or two actions in each category that you can take today to bring you closer to your goal.

Your Daily Goals

Personal Growth

_____

_____

_____

_____

Career

_____

_____

_____

_____

Relationships

_____

_____

_____

_____

Financial

_____

_____

_____

_____

Physical

_____

_____

_____

_____

Spiritual

_____

_____

_____

_____

I make it a habit of doing this balancing exercise every morning before I do anything else. I suggest you give it a try, too. For thirty days, write out your daily goals every morning before you launch into your day. You will be surprised how it helps you prioritize your day better than any to-do list you have utilized in the past. It has done wonders for me. This takes discipline, but if you can make it part of your daily routine, you will bring

> *When you discipline yourself to do the things you need to do, when you need to do them, the day will come when you can do the things you want to do when you want to do them.*
>
> *– Zig Ziglar*

joy, harmony, and peace into your life.

It's funny how those things are all connected—joy, harmony, and peace—and they are direct benefits of the balance you choose to create in your daily activities.

> *One man cannot do right in one department of life whilst he is occupied doing wrong in any other department. Life is one indivisible whole.*
>
> **—Mahatma Gandhi**

Sometimes this exercise is met with resistance. You may say, "I just don't have time for this nonsense. I have so much to do, and now you're giving me MORE exercises to fit in?! I just can't do it all."

You're exactly right.

You can't do it all.

Therefore, use this exercise as a tool to take control of your time. Decide what activities will give you the most balance in your life and prioritize them.

The point of the action is to target exactly where you are depleting your resources. It will save you time rather than wasting your precious minutes. If you're too busy *being* busy, you might miss out on exactly what could give you happiness and fulfillment in life. This exercise helps you define where you need better balance and then gives you an opportunity to make smarter choices about what you will do today to balance your life.

Everyone has their own definition of balance. What might be important to you may not be to someone else. Evaluate each area of your life and thoughtfully consider where you might be able to improve.

Take inventory today, and you will see where you spend your time and energy. How does your list line up with your personal goals and core beliefs?

Knowledge is power. Congratulations on taking this empowering step toward success in every area of your life.

———————— **FINDING THE TIME** ————————

*A*nother very important step to take when you
decide to live a better, less crazy life is to find
out what happens to your time. Are you one of those
people who looks around at the end of the day and
says, "Hey, where did the time go? I never have enough
minutes in the day to get everything done!"

You're not alone. When it comes to time management, some of us are better at it than others. If you are
not a person who manages time well, though, you're
not off the hook!

Just as some people have tidier homes than others
do, some of us really know how to make the most of
our time. It's a gift. However, just as cleaning house
can be taught to anyone, time management is a skill
that we can all learn.

Here are some of the basics:

1. Plan Ahead

One of the prime characteristics of the chronically disorganized is complete and utter surprise when a deadline suddenly arrives.

These people may have even seen the date on a syllabus, memo, email, or other written format but did not process the information thoroughly. This lack of attention to detail may cause missing important deadlines, and that is not good. What a horrible feeling to realize that a big project is due in two hours, and nothing has even been started!!

> *Things which matter most must never be at the mercy of things which matter least.*
>
> **—Johann Wolfgang Von Goethe**

When you receive a due date of any kind, one of the basic rules of time management is to make a written note of that date on your personal calendar.

Note: you can diligently write everything in your calendar and still drop the ball. There are two sub-steps in this method of planning ahead, and the second one is that you actually have to refer to your calendar regularly. Writing everything in a calendar you do not look at will not be particularly useful. Use the calendar on your smartphone, tablet, laptop, or email program so that you can even set reminders and flags when important dates loom.

Write it down first, and then refer to it often as the deadline gets closer.

2. Plan Backwards

Even when you note important deadlines, it is not uncommon to glance at your calendar the day before something is expected and find it to be an unpleasant surprise.

Think about all of the preparation you will need to complete this activity, and get it into the schedule, too.

Check each date as you enter it into your schedule to see if additional preparation or effort is necessary and how long that will take.

Then, make additional dates in your calendar prior to the final date for the advance preparation. That way, you will not be caught off-guard right before an important deadline.

3. Take Note

You can studiously make note of every deadline in the world and add helpful preparation dates to properly spread out your work, but if you do not see the information, none of these actions will help.

> *A marginal plan worked wholeheartedly will work better than a dynamic plan worked half-heartedly.*
>
> **—Zig Ziglar**

You must develop a new protocol—a new daily strategy that incorporates your calendar into your daily routine. One of your first tasks in the morning should be to check your calendar. Look at the day, the week, the month, and then plan out your day accordingly. This will give you plenty of opportunity to add in necessary preparation to complete big deadlines on time and also work those larger tasks in and around your ordinary daily activities.

In fact, I use a strategy in the mornings called "The Power of Three." I pick only three items that I want to accomplish for the day, rather than creating a list of twenty to-dos that I likely won't complete. Instead, focusing on only three items, I can be certain to get those things done and ensure I'm getting my top three goals underway for the day. I personally like to write those three things down on a sticky pad sheet of paper, cross them off as I accomplish them, and then throw away that sheet when I'm done, starting over with a fresh sheet and three new tasks the next day.

Time management extends past simply knowing when something is due. It includes taking note of the big picture and how all of your deadlines fit together.

4. Get Specific

Use your daily calendar not only for the big deadlines, but also to manage your day-to-day tasks. This will help you get better control over your time.

Calculate how much time each task will take, and rank your tasks from most important to least important. Then, enter that information into your calendar and set alarms accordingly.

Life happens, and sometimes an unplanned task will sidetrack you and take over a few hours of your day.

However, if you have completed the most important tasks on your list first, you won't be completely derailed. You can shuffle the less important jobs to the next day, if necessary.

When you get specific and include both the big and the small tasks on the same calendar, you have a stronger overall picture of what you need to accomplish during the day, and you are better equipped to make adjustments as necessary.

5. Plan to Waste Time

Few of us are able to be completely productive all day long. We want to be efficient, but we're not robots. There will be wasted time, so why not plan for it?

Once every few hours, schedule 15 to 20 minutes of "free time." Everyone needs a chance to relax for a moment. Use this time to allow yourself to get distracted. This ends up saving time, believe it or not. If you know you have some free time coming up, you are more likely to stay focused on the task at hand, rather than checking Facebook and responding to personal email.

The truth is that these little distractions are refreshing and necessary, so go ahead and plan them into your day. Enjoy your free time. You deserve it! Then, settle back down to work when the time is up.

Time management is a skill like any other. The more you practice skills to help you manage your time, the more time you will find.

.

— Linking Time to Productivity —

*T*ime management and productivity go hand in hand. If you are not great at one, chances are you could stand a little improvement in the other area, as well.

But don't worry. Both are skills you can improve through practice and following a few tips. It's a lot like exercise. The more you exercise, the better shape you will be in. You don't have to be an Olympic athlete right off the bat. Just keep practicing, and you will improve every day. Your body will become more and more efficient in responding to the task at hand.

Productivity works under the same principle. If you start and maintain a new time management regime, you will see your productivity increase over time. It just takes practice.

Here are a few tips to get you started:

1. Go Big

The professional world is filled with meetings,

deadlines, projects, and travel plans. This can become confusing and overwhelming if you do not learn how to manage your time efficiently.

> *Do your best work so you are seen as a producer.*
>
> **—Unknown**

Start by using a computer program, email schedule, or even a calendar app that allows you to look at months and weeks as well as days. If you'd like to know what I personally use for my calendar system, email us at Info@PrincePerformance.com.

Then, fill out the calendar for as far into the future as you can with the dates of upcoming events. Continue to add new information, even if it is months away.

When you have all of that information at your fingertips, you can look at the entire month on your calendar and get a big-picture view of what is coming up.

Go big, and see how much faster you move toward your goals.

2. Go Small

Once you have a big picture view of your schedule for the next few months, go back in and add important dates by week.

You may already have some of these dates in your calendar from the previous exercise, but you can add more detail now. If you need extra time to prepare for a certain meeting or project, add in a date to start preparing; a date at which you should be halfway prepared;

and, of course, the final deadline.

3. Go Smaller

Next, look at the calendar one day at a time. Add in your scheduled appointments, meetings, and any other personal items like doctor appointments or your kids' soccer games. As an official "soccer mom" of two boys, I can tell you that it is very important to be there for the soccer games, so put them on the schedule!

When you go smaller and add that everyday detail into your calendar, you won't be surprised by things that do take time in your schedule. It's harder to wonder where the minutes go when you have everything down in black and white.

4. Go Personal

You will like this one! Go back into your calendar once again and add some personal time for yourself. Add regular breaks throughout particularly busy days to give yourself the chance to relax, go for a little walk, answer some personal email, or see what the newest celebrity news is online. This will be guilt-free time to indulge in a little bit of rest and relaxation.

It may seem counterproductive, but allowing your brain the chance to relax and coast for a little bit actually boosts your productivity. It allows you to come back more focused and less likely to get distracted later on.

5. Go Global

This is your opportunity to step back and take a look at the global picture. If your calendar program allows you to print, print out the daily, weekly, and monthly schedule for the next three months and take a good look at the events scheduled there.

How does it look from a distance? Step back and see where things get hairy and where you will have more breathing room.

Highlight the events that are particularly important, and then go back into your calendar program and flag those events. Give yourself that advance warning for when big occasions are coming up.

In addition, if the calendar seems far too busy on certain days, this is your chance to delegate. Delegation is a great time management skill. You really don't get a gold star for doing it all. If you can get a helping hand now and then, do it!

Problems are likely to arise in the spots where your calendar is overloaded. Make an effort to delegate where you can and move items around where you can to spread out your tasks into more manageable chunks.

6. Go Over It

This is probably the most important note when it comes to using a calendar to manage time and boost productivity. Go to your calendar often, and keep it up to date.

If a meeting is canceled, change it immediately in

your calendar. If something bumps up or pushes back, change it accordingly.

Your calendar stops working as a tool for productivity if it's not up to date. In fact, it can become a liability if it does not contain accurate, timely information. You will only be productive if you know exactly what is coming up and can manage your time appropriately.

Remember, true productivity is linked to solid time management skills. Get a handle on your time management, and your productivity will begin to rise as a result.

— Linking Productivity to Focus —

*M*ost of us need to be productive. After all, our jobs—and even our daily lives—require it. Without productivity, deadlines pass, the refrigerator empties out, meetings get missed, and the people around us become frustrated with our inefficiency.

So productivity is important. We established in the last chapter that time management is linked to productivity. Now, let me show you how productivity is linked to focus.

We all want to be productive. It is a trait we desire but rarely achieve. If we do manage to be productive, it isn't very consistent. It

> *Laziness may appear attractive, but work gives satisfaction.*
>
> **—Anne Frank**

comes in spurts in between moments of distraction.

Oh, and aren't those distractions delicious these days! We have the joys of technology, the Internet, Netflix, social media, apps, chatting with coworkers and friends, email, voicemail, texting, or simply doing whatever we can to avoid the mundane part of work.

I admit it, I fall prey to distractions all the time, too. We all do. We're not perfect. We like distractions. But think of it this way: if you learn to focus and increase your productivity, then you will have more time for the yummy distractions of life. So let me give you a few tips, and if you follow them, you just might end up with extra time at the end of the day to play.

You will find that your productivity will improve significantly through some basic, easy lifestyle changes that will help you focus. Increasing your focus will help you get organized in such a way that your daily tasks will not seem so overwhelming.

Try these simple changes to your routine, and observe what happens to your productivity:

1. Start Early

Whether you are a morning person or not, the fact of the matter is that adding an hour or two to your day can make a dramatic difference.

In fact, if you decide to complete just one task early in the morning, before you do anything else, you will increase your productivity in the first few hours of the day and set the tone for the rest of the day, as well.

The task you choose to complete early in the morning does not necessarily have to be work-related. What items on your list do you find it hard to fit in during the day?

Have you been skipping workouts on a regular basis, because other activities are taking up much of your time? Get up an hour earlier and check exercise off the list before everyone else even gets out of bed. It is incredibly empowering to do that for yourself, whether you are a morning person or not. If it becomes part of your routine and increases your overall health and happiness, you just might discover you enjoy mornings.

2. Prioritize

Prioritizing the events in your day is a great way to focus your attention where it is needed and therefore increase productivity.

Every evening before you go to bed, look at your schedule for the next day. Run down your list of tasks for the day, and prioritize them from most important to least important.

Block in the times when your presence is required at a meeting or other event, and then sprinkle the tasks in between all of the static events. Remember to put in the most important tasks first, just in case you don't get to everything.

It only takes a few minutes to do this at the end of the day, and then you will wake up the next morning with a clear sense of what to focus on when.

I urge you to try this simple tip. You will be surprised by how quickly it improves your productivity and also gets you going in the morning. You don't have to waste any time deciding what to do. It's all already laid out for you.

3. Focus

There are so many tiny distractions in the day that becoming a master in the art of multitasking is gaining in popularity. Unfortunately, the truth is multitasking does not really help you with productivity.

If you try to do more than one thing at a time, you will not get points for time management. Instead, you will have a tendency to slow down and do both tasks poorly.

Instead, pick one task to work on at a time, and focus exclusively on that task. Your work will be better for it and so will your productivity.

It may be hard to remain focused on one task at first, but you can do it. Practice focus. Resist the urge to stop and check your email or play a game on your iPhone. Save those tasks for your 15 to 20 minutes of free time.

4. Close the Door

The sociable nature of offices and homes these days means that there is always something going on somewhere. People want to talk, the dog needs to be walked, someone in the office is having a birthday, your daughter just spilled juice on the floor in the kitchen. There are all kinds of distractions flying around you constantly like little gnats, vying for your attention. And you probably want to be part of most of them. We're social creatures. We like to be in the middle of what's going on.

However, when it's time to complete a task, it is important to filter out as many distractions as possible in order to get that task done—and then have time left over to be social.

One very easy way to shut out distractions is literally to close the door. If possible, complete your work in a room with a door that you can shut. Do not answer the phone or stop to check emails. Stay focused on the task. You will finish it much more efficiently if you are able to hold your focus. Then, you can open the door to the outside world again.

If you work in a cubicle or in a home office space that does not have a door, quiet is harder to come by, but it is possible. Invest in a set of headphones and listen to quiet music while you work. The headphones will show others that you do not wish to be disturbed, and you will be able to focus on the job at hand until you are done with your task.

5. Get Talking

This last tip may surprise you. We tend to think all of the technology we have available to us today should make us more efficient and productive, but that is not always the case.

We now have multiple ways of getting in touch with someone. We can call, email, text, instant message, Facebook, Tweet, or use a host of other social media. But which one is the fastest?

You may be shocked to find that a quick phone

conversation is almost always more efficient than any other form of communication. You may compose and respond to three or four emails before you get all of the information you need, but a phone call could have taken care of the details in a couple of minutes.

Texting is much more than typing out a short, cryptic message. It is usually followed by continual glances at the phone to see if there was a response and to type out an answer to that response.

Studies are still coming out about the time we lose typing messages on various keyboards rather than having a real-time conversation.

I urge you to give that ancient device called the phone a try and find out if it saves you some time. You may increase your productivity by calling people back instead of being pulled into email conversations or texts.

Set aside a few times a day to make and respond to calls, and ask people to call you instead of using email or text messaging to make the message clear. You may be amazed by how much time you save.

So give these few simple tips a try, and you may be surprised by how an increase in focus will link to higher productivity.

1. Start early to give yourself an extra hour or two in the day.
2. Prioritize your tasks the night before, so you can focus on an efficient schedule the minute you're

ready to go in the morning.

3. Focus on one thing at a time, and you will complete more items on your list than you would if you tried multitasking.

4. Close the door to outside distractions, and open the door to an increase in focus and productivity.

5. Use the phone. It will often get the job done faster than emailing or texting.

You can make a real difference in your productivity by linking it to focus. Intensify your focus, and see how fast you complete your tasks for the day. Focus is lightening in a bottle, and it will ultimately free up more time and give you the flexibility to better balance your life.

Stop Wasting It

N o doubt about it, spending time on social media websites, texting friends and family, surfing the web, and playing games on your smartphone is
fun. In fact, it usually beats actual work tasks and other
obligations by far.

It's fun to waste time. Some might even call it addictive. After all, it provides instant gratification, and it's
enjoyable. Most of us tend to choose wasting time over
focusing on our responsibilities, even though we're
embarrassed to admit it. It's like putting a hot fudge
sundae and a bowl of spinach in front of a five year old.
Which one do you think they will choose?

As a result of our indulgences, our time management
is a mess. We spend our days feeling frantic and behind
schedule, and it's our own fault, but we seldom admit
it. We like to blame it on being so BUSY.

"If I wasn't so *busy*, I wouldn't feel so crazy all the
time."

"I'm so *busy*! I have too many responsibilities, too

much on my plate."

Is that really true? Or are we wasting the time we do have?

In this chapter, I will hand over one last key to time management. It's a very important one. If you could see it, it would probably be very big and gold and shiny. The true key to time management (drum roll please):

Stop wasting time.

I know, I know, that wasn't a very exciting answer.

But it's true. Stop wasting time. Really. It's not rocket science.

I feel like I just let the air out of your tires when I gave you that bit of information. I'm sorry. It's a bummer, isn't it?

Twitter is fun! You enjoy watching TV. What about the happiness part of this whole "balance" thing?

> *Opportunities are usually disguised by hard work, so most people don't recognize them.*
>
> **—Ann Landers**

You may even take your addictive behavior one step further. "I'm still getting my job done...eventually," you say. "I made it to all my meetings yesterday."

Sure, you did the bare minimum. Maybe you squeaked by. But did you do the best you could do with the work that was in front of you? Are you proud of what you did, or did you just get it done as haphazardly as possible, so you could play on the Internet?

I sound like a mother, don't I?

Well, I am a mother, so I guess that's okay.

But honestly, I feel the same way. I want to have my cake and eat it too. However, this book is about productivity. It's about doing more in less time and achieving your goals and following your dreams. You can't do all that if you're not willing to put in the work.

Unfortunately, if you are willing to put in the work, you also have to be willing to stop wasting time. Don't worry! You don't have to quit the Internet cold turkey. But you do have to limit your time in cyberspace—that is if you want to truly live a fulfilling life and follow your real passion.

Ask yourself what components in your life really deserve your full attention. Your business projects and deadlines need your attention and deserve quality work. Your coworkers deserve to have your full attention and assistance. Your loved ones deserve your undivided attention when you spend time with them. The sad truth is, about the only thing that does not need your full attention is wasting time on the Internet.

As you progress throughout your day, utilize that magic word: **focus**.

Focus on each thing you do. Give it everything you've got. Do just that one thing. Remove or stop distractions from other sources, so that you are giving your full attention to the task. Refuse to be disturbed unless it is an emergency. Then, once you have finished that task, start the next one. You will snowball into productivity.

Here's the good news: if you need to add time into your schedule to check your social updates, then schedule it in once or twice a day. Pick a time when you do not need to be accomplishing other things. Then, go for it! Get that social media fix, or whatever you need, without work distractions. After you give yourself a little fun time, you will feel more relaxed and satisfied, instead of feeling secretive or anxious because you really should be finishing that work project instead of wasting time watching the online world go by.

Try delaying the gratification that you get from wasting time. Perhaps the first few days you can reward your new attempt at better time management by putting in some free time two times a day and once when you are back at home at the end of the day. After a few days, reduce it to just once during the workday and once in the evening. In a few weeks, try removing it from your office time, but enjoy an hour or two of surfing the web at home after dinner.

Find a time in your schedule when the fun stuff does not interfere with any other obligations, and you can enjoy it freely. This is all part of the balancing act you are perfecting. The rest of your day will have been a marvel of efficiency and time management, and you will get gratification from that, as well. It is, as they say, a total win-win.

ATTACKING YOUR NEMESIS

*N*ow that you're through wasting time, you are ready to attack the to-do list. The dreaded to-do list is an immortal nemesis that everyone has to do battle with on a daily basis. But you can turn this struggle into a choreographed dance instead of a full-out brawl when you utilize smart organization and time management tactics. If you have trouble taking control of your growing list of pending tasks, try some of these tactics to get a better grip on your to-do's.

Make Prioritized Lists

Lists are a great friend to many busy people. Without an organized, written plan for the pending tasks in your life, it's easy to forget an important element. While any list is better than no list, there are some great strategies you can use to make yours as efficient as possible.

The first strategy is to divide and conquer. Prioritize your to-do list in a variety of ways—especially if it is very long.

Begin by separating your list into several shorter lists for each area of your life. You may have lists for work, home, and hobbies. On each list, prioritize your items into categories like A, B, and C, for their level of importance; or give each item its own number from top to bottom, so you know how they rank by importance or urgency.

Finally, if you want to become a time management guru with your to-do lists, you can assign due dates to the tasks. Then, you will know at a glance which ones are time sensitive and which ones can wait a few days.

Plan Scheduled Steps

If you're staring down the barrel at a big project, it's often nearly impossible to see the first few steps in light of the monumental end picture you're striving to achieve. Instead of panicking, find that first step and take it. Refrain from looking at the whole for a little while and only concentrate on one small step at a time. Pretty soon, you will discover that you are making great progress.

> *Whether you think you can or think you can't, you're right.*
>
> **—Henry Ford**

If you are fearful of not ever making it through a project, write out every step that needs to be completed along the way, and schedule each one individually into your calendar. Make these steps as small as needed to seem manageable. This is a time management tactic that makes even the biggest projects achievable.

You will be able to look at your calendar every day and track your progress. You will also never lose sight of the finish line—the point where you will finally complete your task.

Integrate Technology

Technology is both a friend and an enemy to efficient time management. When you let it act as a distraction, it can be difficult to overcome. When you use technology to your advantage, however, it can be a very useful tool.

Keeping organized lists, reminders, and a calendar on your smart phone will ensure that you have time management tools on hand everywhere you go. If you are waiting on an appointment, you can even use your phone, tablet, or laptop, to make the most of this time and get more done with portable office tools.

The best time management tactics will vary with the individual. Look for tactics that fit your lifestyle and organizational preferences, and implement these new strategies to keep track of your to-do list. It will feel great when you get into a rhythm of steadily checking off those pending items.

We have gone over many tips in these first few chapters to help you streamline the skills in your balancing act. You have been learning lots of new ways to increase productivity and focus.

In the next chapter, you will have a chance to evaluate your productivity and target areas for further improvement.

— Evaluating Your Productivity —

*P*roductivity is an important issue for every business, but this crucial factor can be difficult to quantify. In this chapter, we will look at ways to evaluate productivity.

As an employee, you want to make sure that you can show measurable productivity to your employer. You never know when difficult financial times may cause employers to take a closer look at productivity within their business and consider cutting jobs. Therefore, it's important to be able to show your productivity and ensure that your position is truly valuable to the company.

As an employer, you must be able to evaluate productivity to ensure that your company is operating as efficiently as possible. It is essential to know whether or not you are doing everything you can to increase productivity and lower costs while still maintaining your standards.

Set the Scale

While it's difficult to accurately measure something as changeable as productivity on a finite scale, setting up a system for productivity evaluations will give everyone a benchmark to measure their work against. A system of measuring productivity is also important so that every employee knows exactly what is expected of them, and they have the opportunity to meet or exceed those goals.

In some departments, productivity may be measurable in easily quantifiable numbers, such as time on the phone for customer service, or a dollar amount in sales.

In other areas, it will take a little more creativity to define productivity. Determine how much you value each part of the work process, and use that valuation to set the scale. One employee may complete faster data entry, while another is slower but much more precise. Which do you value more—speed or accuracy? A careful balance between quality and quantity must always be maintained.

Set a scale for each department or job position to measure productivity against. If you're looking to measure your own personal productivity, set specific goals that you need to meet each day and week, and measure your actual success against your ideal productivity goals.

Determine Methods of Measurement

Once you've decided what is to be expected of each individual, you should decide how you will keep track of productivity. The best way to accurately evaluate someone's true productivity is to look at the averages over a long period of time. Any company can have a bad week with lots of unexpected problems that slow things down, or even a particularly good week where things go much better than expected. Tracking productivity over time will even out those valleys and peaks and give you a better average.

By looking at long-term averages, you will get a clear and accurate picture of productivity in a certain area of the company. As you evaluate the results, you will likely find many areas for improvement as well as areas for praise. Don't forget to offer praise when it is earned! Then, recalibrate your methods of measurement from time to time, so no area of the company is allowed to stagnate.

There will always be ways to improve productivity, so constantly tweak your methods of measurement and your methods of increasing productivity. This will help your business continue to grow and thrive.

Consider Mitigating Factors

When there's a sharp decrease in productivity, it's important to track down its true source. Poor productivity isn't always the fault of the employee, and there may be steps you can take to better equip various departments. Your productivity evaluations should always come with a built-in space for noting any mitigating factors. Whether it's a holiday break where most clients are out of the office, making sales difficult, or a natural disaster that slowed down deliveries, there are a lot of unexpected events that can have a major impact on the bottom line of productivity.

Encourage everyone in your company to view productivity as an ongoing project that can always be improved. Remember that productivity isn't always about numbers. Even when you're churning out the maximum number of reports each week, there's still room to polish the quality or improve the production process. In business, you must always look forward to the next way to get better.

–Tricks for Dealing with Deadlines–

*J*ust as evaluating productivity is an integral part of any good business, deadlines are also unavoidable in business. You simply can't have a smoothly running company without deadlines for all of the essential tasks that keep everything moving forward.

Unfortunately, deadlines are often seen as troublesome and stressful instead of useful and important. If you have trouble dealing with deadlines, try these tactics to make them more manageable.

Break the Deadlines Down

When you get a deadline for a big project, you should immediately break that end goal down into a series of smaller deadlines. If you have a big report due on Friday, don't blindly scramble forward with Friday on the edge of your mind. Instead, give yourself a break. Map out at all the little steps that must be taken to get you there, and you will more clearly see your path to completion in manageable chunks.

For example, you could plan to have your research done by Tuesday afternoon, a rough draft completed by the end of the day on Wednesday, and the final report completed by Thursday. When you aim to get your project done early, you're building your own extension into the schedule. You don't have to ask a superior for another twenty-four hours. You already provided for that extra day in your own time management plan.

Finishing early will ensure that you don't turn in a hastily done project without giving it the attention, fine tuning, and final polish that it needs. When you're done early, you also have time to sleep on it. You might think of one more way to tweak it in the morning, and then finish with results that you're truly proud of.

Act Smart, Not Fast

If you get too focused on your deadline, you may end up prioritizing fast action. Everything you think about relating to the project suddenly has to do with speed rather than accuracy.

However, all your time and effort will be for naught if you're moving in the wrong direction. It's always worth the extra time to do your research and make sure you're implementing the right plan of action. Act smart, not fast, no matter what the deadline.

Just about every important business project begins with research before action. Don't let a pending deadline spur you into action before you're ready. The first step with any project is laying out a plan. When you take your time on this, you will ensure that your time is well-managed throughout.

Stop Checking the Clock

When you have a big deadline looming, it's tempting to glance at the clock every few minutes to see how you're coming along. Will you make it in time?

Unfortunately, constantly checking the time is a time waster all its own. You're never going to get into the groove of churning out high quality work when your mind is really on the seconds ticking by.

Set your phone aside, put the clock out of sight, and focus completely on the task at hand when you're struggling with a deadline. Perform one job at a time, and never let yourself get sucked into multitasking, no matter how much is going on. When you do two tasks at once, both will take longer and get poorer results. Do one task at a time with focused dedication, and you'll end up with extra time to spend on the other projects on your list.

> *When you get hold of a project, you really need to get after it... Then when you get it going, all you have to do is keep that easy, steady pressure!*
>
> **—Zig Ziglar**

Dealing with deadlines doesn't have to be difficult. Break your projects up into manageable steps, take the time to put together a good action plan, and give your project focused attention. With these easy tactics, you'll be able to beat any deadline with time to spare and reliably deliver high quality results.

———— PRODUCTIVITY PITFALLS ————

*W*e've talked a lot so far about the positive side of productivity, but it has its dark side, too. Productivity is a tricky beast that can trip you up in many subtle ways. When you have your eyes on a big goal, there are many smaller things that can sabotage you below the radar. Keep an eye out for these productivity pitfalls and make a note of how you can avoid them.

Too Much Time Spent Planning

There's a fine line between appropriate time management and over-managing your every task. Making a to-do list once is great, but spending hours categorizing, color coding, and editing your list just ends up wasting time that could be spent checking things off of it.

Avoid it: Come up with a well-organized plan for managing your schedule, deadlines, and task list, and stick to it. Spend a minimal amount of time planning how you'll get things done, and instead focus on actually doing them. Over-planning is a big enemy of productivity.

Too Much Overtime

Working extra hours is an easy habit to fall into, and at first it will give your productivity a major boost. Riding the thrill of all those check marks on your to-do list can spur you to continue with long nights and working weekends. Over time, this will actually have a negative impact on your productivity levels.

Avoid it: Maintain a reasonable schedule as often as possible, and leave overtime for extreme situations. Refreshed, relaxed business owners and employees always perform better over the long term.

Multitasking

While many employees pride themselves on their ability to do several things at once, this really isn't a good thing. When you multitask, you give a fraction of your attention to several tasks at once, rather than giving all of your attention to the project at hand. Multitasking is an enemy of productivity and not a point of pride.

Avoid it: Set aside distractions and work on one thing at a time to boost your productivity levels. When possible, avoid checking your phone and email constantly while you're in the middle of a task.

Rocky Workplace Relationships

Your relationships with others in the workplace may have a very big impact on your productivity. If you're uncomfortable with a coworker and avoid him or her, you may be sabotaging projects where that individual's input would be useful. Failure to work together and communicate freely will slow down your work.

Avoid it: When you have the opportunity, cultivate strong working relationships with your colleagues, so you're able to be as productive as possible in every area.

With these pitfalls in mind, you will be equipped to avoid the temptations that can ruin your productivity and take advantage of all the tools at your disposal to get the maximum amount of work done.

Next, we will move on to the 80/20 principle to zero in even closer to the most important aspects of productivity.

— Leveraging the 80/20 Principle —

*A*nyone who has ever tried to manage their day has encountered the fact that the most productive time is usually the result of a small piece of concentrated effort, and much of the rest of the time is frittered away with only minimal accomplishments. Often stated as the 80/20 principle, 80 percent of the accomplishment is a result of 20 percent of the time spent. Conversely, 20 percent of the accomplishments that occur are a result of actions that take up 80 percent of your time.

Sometimes the 80/20 principle is likened to the Pareto Principle, which is applied to projects where the majority of progress is accomplished in the smaller time expended. The Pareto Principle is actually a formal statistical process that helps identify the causes of time consuming problems and helps to make

> *In the field of human endeavor, 80 percent of the results flow from 20 percent of the activities.*
>
> **– Pareto**

> *The significant prob-*
> *lems we face cannot*
> *be solved at the same*
> *level of thinking we*
> *were at when we*
> *created them.*
>
> **—Albert Einstein**

any process more efficient. You can use the same principle to analyze your own activities and schedule to find where the 20 percent is concentrated and where 80 percent of your time is expended.

In your own day-to-day world, however, managing your time will help to uncover where you are wasting it. The purpose is to find those time-consuming activities that only produce 20 percent of the results. The analysis is a valuable exercise that can make you a more productive person.

Start with Analysis

Start by analyzing where you actually spend your time. Keep a diary for a couple of weeks to determine what activities take how much time, and measure the productive output from those hours.

You will probably find that a large portion of your daily activities are very unproductive.

Go for Maximum Impact

With a solid record of where your time is actually spent, the question becomes how do you limit those activities and concentrate on those things that really have an impact.

To reduce the impact of unproductive activities on

your day, start by creating a daily schedule. Literally schedule every activity that you need to account for. Your schedule might be the same every day, or it may constantly change, or it might be somewhere in between the two. It depends completely on your line of work. Some businesses have staff meetings every Monday; others schedule events to flow with sales or other milestones. It doesn't really matter whether your days are uniform or very different. What matters is that you track your activity.

> *The formulation of a problem is far more often essential than its solution, which may be merely a matter of mathematical or experimental skill.*
>
> **—Albert Einstein**

Once you have created a daily schedule, set aside special time for the heart of your activities. Sales people, for example, need to set aside time for cold calling potential customers. Then, they may set aside some time for follow-ups on recent sales. Finally, they might put in some time to listen to subordinates. Create a block of time for each activity, and minimize or eliminate those activities that are time killers. You are always going for maximum impact in a minimal amount of time when you create your schedule.

Follow Your Schedule

Start off every day by following your own schedule, and stick with it until the day is completed. What you will find is that you can complete your job in less time than you think, and you can even set aside time for a little bit of fun.

If you like golf, schedule it in, but not at the expense of those activities that have proven to be productive. If you follow this advice and follow your schedule, you will not only complete the functions that need to be finished, but you will also give yourself guilt-free time for those recreational or social activities that you have always wanted to include in your schedule.

You will never be able to get around the problem that some events on your schedule will be less productive than others. However, minimizing the time allocated to more unproductive activities and concentrating on those things that produce results will boost your overall productivity and move you to the center ring in the balancing act.

−How Highly Effective People Do It−

*H*ow do successful people bring all of this information on productivity and focus together in a way that works? How do they manage their jobs and their everyday lives in a way that is so balanced and healthy?

Here are some of their habits that you can adopt for yourself.

Create a daily schedule.

Creating a daily schedule and then actually following that daily plan is the single most important habit that you can learn. Create a plan for yourself, and stick to it.

Time management is the control of your most valuable asset—time—and it will ultimately be the factor that determines your success. Time management determines where you

> *People who don't know what cannot be done often go ahead and do it.*
>
> **—Zig Ziglar**

put your effort and how you spend your most important resource.

Give the most important activities the highest priority.

You already know at a glance where the most important tasks appear on your calendar. They should be in prominent positions.

> *The key is not to prioritize your schedule but to schedule our priorities.*
>
> —Stephen R. Covey

Sales personnel need to sell. Every single day, priority must be given to contacting potential clients and following up on recent orders. Other professions have their list of top priorities, too. They have important activities that are always on the top of the list.

Make important activities your highest priority. They should always be the most important things on your daily schedule. Place them in a time slot where they cannot be avoided. Early in the day may be best for some. Others will have specific times set aside that work for them. Always, always, always schedule these important activities first, and do not avoid them just because they make you nervous.

Leave some time for learning and stay up-to-date on the industry.

Remember to leave some time for longer term goals.

Put a portion of your schedule into keeping up with the industry, the profession, or the company. Read current materials, attend a class, or talk with your colleagues in other organizations.

Staying up-to-date in your industry and continually studying it is a valuable habit that should be included in your daily schedule, perhaps once a week.

Follow the schedule every day.

Another key habit to get into is to never allow yourself to lapse into lazy planning. Keep your schedule active and up to date.

Start every day by following the activity you have scheduled. It is this constant commitment to a schedule that creates the most important element of time management—consistency. Make success a habit by following your schedule every day.

Measure your success.

As you conduct your daily plan, keep track of where you are successful. The goal of this exercise is to know what time is spent on the most productive outcomes.

Keep track of sales, solved computer program bugs, improved shipping problems, or whatever is your primary function. Make measuring success a habit, and you will be able to speak knowledgeably when it comes time to

> *We first make our habits, then our habits make us.*
>
> **– Anonymous**

speak up for your team.

Re-calibrate your schedule based on success.

As you can measure how well your plan is working, regularly go back and re-examine if you are spending your time on the right activities.

If you find that one activity worked better than another, give the successful task more time. You now have the tools to constantly re-calibrate your schedule based on your successes. Don't let this valuable data go to waste. Use it to improve your productivity.

Leave some time for recreation or relaxation.

When all is said and done, you need to schedule some time for recreation. It is just as important as the time you schedule for sales and project meetings.

> *Success qualities are learned and developed.*
>
> —Zig Ziglar

When you have a good plan, you can easily include time for recreation that does not impact the time that you need to spend following your job and career. It will give you the energy to accomplish the goals that you have set elsewhere.

Make it a habit to spend some of your time away from the daily grind. You will return balanced, refreshed, and ready to take on the next task before you.

— Overcoming Procrastination —

*P*rocrastination is the last big, scary item that will thwart your efforts at a balanced and happy life. It may look like a sloth, but it is a dangerous beast and will kill all of the efforts you've made so far to stop juggling and start getting more done in less time.

Let's look procrastination right in the eye and blast it out of your life!

Start with a short self-evaluation. Think back over the last year, and ask yourself the following questions:

- When have I procrastinated?
- What didn't I complete because I put off doing the work I needed to do?
- What were the consequences?

Now, as you are thinking through those times when procrastination kept you from reaching your goal, don't beat yourself up too much. Procrastination is a problem for many, many people.

But there are ways to fight procrastination and win. I'm going to give you some great weapons to win your battle against procrastination in this chapter.

Zig Ziglar is a big proponent of setting goals. He is always asking: What do you want to be? What do you want to do? What do you want to have?

I have learned a lot from his leadership. In the Prince household, we have a tradition around setting goals. (I'll admit right now that I may have forced this tradition at first, since I am the one who is into personal

> *Sow a thought, reap an action;*
> *Sow an action, reap a habit;*
> *Sow a habit, reap a character;*
> *Sow a character, reap a destiny.*
>
> **– Samuel Smiles**

development in our family.) Every New Year's Eve, we gather around, and each of us gets a piece of paper to write down five personal goals for the coming year— five things we want to be; five things we want to do; five things we want to have. We all do this, even my kids.

We started this tradition when my oldest son was four years old, and their goals when they were little were kind of sweet and funny sometimes. They would list things like going roller skating, making the soccer team, or going to Disney World. But throughout the year, when they would accomplish one of their goals, we would go to their room where the list was posted and check that goal off the list. It gave all of us a terrific sense of accomplishment.

We repeated the exercise as a family, too. As a family,

what do we want to be? What do we want to do? What do we want to have? We worked toward our collective goals and grew as a family.

When my son was six years old, he said something that completely blew me away. It was the day he realized he had met all five goals he had written down for the year.

"Mom, this is so cool!" he said. "All you have to do is write it down, and it happens!"

I got such a kick out of that. We tend to complicate things so much as adults, but this little six year old got it. It was that simple. All we have to do is figure out what we want and write it down. Then, it is much more likely to happen.

Now, leading back to the topic of goals, here is another question:

Why do some people accomplish their goals and others don't?

I am asked this question all the time, and there are many answers.

There are some people who just refuse to take the time to set goals. They think they already know what they want in life, so they shouldn't have to write it down. I can tell you from my years of coaching experience, those are typically the people who don't accomplish any of their goals.

Other people create goals, but their goals are not really tied to their passion or purpose in life. That is exactly why I think it is so important to first discover your passions before you do anything else. If you're not setting goals around something you are truly passionate about, what are the chances you will achieve those goals? You have to tie that in and make sure you look at it very closely before you set your goals.

> *You may be disappointed if you fail, but you are doomed if you don't try.*
>
> **—Beverly Sills**

Another reason people do not accomplish their goals is that they set a goal and never look at it again. I have been guilty of this—I set a goal, put it in the drawer, and then forget about it for months. The goal has to be in a place where you will see it every day, so that you can maintain your focus on achieving it.

There are many, many reasons why people do not achieve their goals, but one reason surpasses all the rest: procrastination.

Procrastination is such a prevalent barrier to reaching your goals. When I speak to groups, I often ask, "How many of you are procrastinators?"

You wouldn't believe the response! People are practically climbing over their chairs to claim this ailment—as if they're proud of it. It's nothing to be proud of, though.

We act like procrastination is some sort of disease that we cannot fight, but think about other aspects of your life. Did you procrastinate checking your email this morning? Did you procrastinate going on Twitter or Facebook? Probably not.

But are you procrastinating getting your work done? What about taking that trip you have always wanted to take? Procrastination is a choice, and we tend to reserve it for the big things. We procrastinate on the things that matter the most; the things that will bring the most joy and satisfaction. It's really silly when you think about it, but that's what we do. We put the important things on the back burner.

Let me tell you, your days of procrastinating are numbered. You are no longer going to wait for someday. I will walk you through a plan right now that will help you overcome procrastination.

There are four steps to removing procrastination from your life:

Step 1: Identify What's Holding You Back

There are legitimate reasons why some people procrastinate. They may have difficulty concentrating or other physical or mental hurdles to overcome. But for most of us, that's not the case.

You might be procrastinating because of fear. Fear of failure, of course, but also fear of succeeding. If you accomplish this goal, then what?

Think about why you are procrastinating. Is it fear? Anxiety? What is holding you back? You have to identify it before you can remove it. Ask yourself: Why am I procrastinating on this? Do I not believe in myself? Do

I think I'm not worth it? What is the negative jabber in my head around this? Am I getting anything positive out of putting this off?

Step 2: Practice Discipline And Motivation

The simple truth is achieving anything worthwhile in your life takes practice. If someone comes up to you and tells you they have an easy way for you to make a million dollars with almost no effort, run! You can achieve anything you want, but it's going to take some work.

That doesn't mean it has to be hard, though.

When you are following your goals and working on something you're passionate about, it doesn't feel like work. It's not hard, because you're right where you want to be.

When I wrote my book, *Winning in Life Now*, I got the inspiration for the book at a live event. I'm a big believer in live events, because being around other people is inspiring. I made the decision at that event to write my book.

So I went home, got out my laptop, and started cranking out that book. In three weeks, I had the entire thing written. Now, it took eight months to get all of the final pieces in place, but the big push only took three weeks. During that time, I stayed up later than I've ever stayed up;

> *You don't invent your mission, you detect it.*
>
> —**Victor Frankl**

I got up earlier than I ever have before; I worked harder than I have ever worked in my life—and I had a full-time job on top of all this! And of course, motherhood never takes a break, either, so I was one busy woman.

It didn't matter. I was working very, very hard, but it wasn't difficult, because the project was pulling me, rather than me pushing the project. It was exhilarating.

If you choose a goal that is aligned with your passion, you will have the same experience. You will have to practice and develop a strong discipline and motivation, but it will not be hard, because your heart will be in it.

Step 3: Dust Off Your Dreams

What do you think would happen if I stood in front of a classroom of kindergarten students and asked them, "What do you want to be when you grow up? What are your dreams?"

They wouldn't hesitate to give their answers. Kids have dreams—big dreams—and they have every intension of making those dreams come true.

Do you remember your dreams? Have you thought about them lately? Dust off those old dreams, if they haven't been out in the light for awhile. Take a second look at them. They will rekindle your passion and help you to move forward in achieving your goals.

I caught a glimpse of my dream when I went to that Zig Ziglar seminar at age eighteen. I didn't even know what passion was back then, but something fired up inside of me when I was around people, successful people, who wanted more out of life. I am just as enthusiastic about this dream today as I was at eighteen.

So remind yourself of your passions. Dust off those dreams, and set goals to achieve them. Nothing strikes procrastination down faster than a passionate person with goals and plans to achieve their dreams.

Step 4: Start Living Now

This one is deceptively simple, but procrastination really boils down to one thing: inaction. If you start living now, you launch into action and thwart evil procrastination. You have to make a conscious decision that you are worth it and then just do it. No waiting. No putting it off. Start living now! Why would you want to wait to realize your dreams and live your passion every day?

I would like to tell you a story about my friend Tom. I also included this story in my book *Winning in Life Now*, because I feel it is such an important illustration.

Tom was in his early forties. He had it all: a wonderful family, young kids in elementary school, a beautiful wife. He was one of those guys who just seemed to do everything right. He ate right, worked out, took good care of himself. He did it all.

So Tom went to his annual doctor's appointment, and his doctor discovered a little lump. They did a bunch of tests, and everything was just a bit off.

"Don't worry about it," the doctor assured him. "I'm

sure it's fine. But let's just do a few more tests to be certain."

About a week later, Tom and his wife received a phone call from the doctor asking them to come back into the office. It didn't sound like he would be giving them terrific news, but nothing could have prepared them for what they heard that day. Not only did Tom have cancer, but it was in Stage IV, and he had six months to live. Six months.

What do you do with that diagnosis?

At first, Tom was mad. He flew through all of the stages of grief.

"This isn't fair!" he ranted. "How could this be happening to me? I did everything right!"

Then the sadness kicked in. "I have kids and a wife. What will happen to my beautiful family when I'm no longer here? I will miss seeing my children grow up. I will not get to grow old with my wife."

And finally, he came to acceptance. He realized that no matter what he did in that moment, he

> *The pain, she passes...but the beauty remains forever.*
>
> **— Renoir**

could not avoid the fact that there was a very good chance he would not be around in a few months.

That's when Tom made a decision. He said, "I'm only going to do the things I really, really love to do, and I'm going to spend whatever days I have left with the people I love the most."

That's exactly what he did. He spent time with his family, enjoying every minute with them. Another thing he loved to do was write. He had put it aside when life got busy with work and family, but in these final months, he started writing at night after his kids went to bed. He wrote letters and stories about what he did with them when they were young. He collected all of those wonderful memories in his words, so that his family could cherish them. It was a legacy that would become very valuable to them in years to come.

Tom died six-and-a-half months after that doctor's appointment. His family was understandably devastated to lose him, but Tom's wife said something to me at the funeral that has stuck with me ever since. It is something that still inspires me to keep going after my goals and do what I love to do.

She said, "Tom came to me about a week before he died and said that he was *grateful* for the prognosis, because without it he never would have experienced what it *really* feels like to live."

That hit me right between the eyes. Why do we need a prognosis of death to get over whatever is holding us back? Why do we need somebody to tell us we're sick before we decide that it's okay to follow our dreams and goals?

> *Life is too short to be ordinary. Start living an extraordinary life now!*
>
> **—Michelle Prince**

Don't wait until you receive a fatal prognosis before you decide to get busy and live. You have an opportunity right now to launch into action, and that is exactly my point when it comes to overcoming procrastination. There is nothing in the world that is more important than your dreams and your goals. But you do have to take action and make it happen. At the end of the day, all you have to do is get started. Take one step.

What works for you may not work for someone else, so you have to find your own path. For me personally, I had to get away from it all. I took a day off of work and got away from distractions of family and business and everything else. That's when I sat down and asked myself, "What do I really want out of life?" In the stillness, I was able to answer.

Start journaling; write down your ideas. Answer the questions I gave you earlier. Find out what it is you want, and then make a commitment to go after it.

There is one thing that many of us never fully realize: you are in control. You make choices every moment that put you exactly where you are today. If you want to be somewhere else, make different choices. You may not particularly like that statement, but the point is, no matter what is going on in your life, you have control over your attitude and your actions. What do you want to accomplish? Find out, and then get busy! Make a commitment to follow your dreams. If you feel held back by responsibilities at work or at home, I urge you to make the commitment anyway—on behalf of your family and your business. You are much more valuable to everyone around you if you are leading a life that inspires them. So if you can't do it for yourself, do it for your family. When you inspire them, they will find the courage to follow your lead.

That's what happened to me when I wrote my first book. Sure, I was proud of the achievement of publishing a book, but there was so much more. I actually changed my kids' lives and so many others who were around me when I accomplished this goal. It had nothing to do with the content of the book. It was because I took action. I put one foot in front of the other and achieved a significant goal in my life. That inspired them to do the same.

> *Try not to become a man of success, rather a man of value.*
>
> **— Albert Einstein**

You can do this, too. You can inspire others. Just make a commitment to yourself. If you can't do that, make a commitment to somebody else. Decide that you are done waiting. Decide you will go after your goals today.

I'm not special. I'm no different than you. I'm a wife, a mom, a friend, a sister; I have a company. I'm busy. I work. So if I can do it; you can do it. And I really truly believe that.

Life is so short. We all have an opportunity to be extraordinary. Don't wait until it's too late to grab on to your opportunity. Don't be ordinary. Take action. Overcome your procrastination, and make this year the best of your life.

— Taking the Act on the Road —

*N*ow you have all the skills you need to take your balancing act on the road. You no longer have to be busy *being* busy. You can throw those juggling balls away. You know exactly how to take all your energy and feed it into a life filled with purpose.

In this book, you have learned about productivity, focus, the 80/20 principle, scheduling your time wisely, measuring your productivity, and avoiding the pitfalls associated with productivity. You have dealt with deadlines and to-do lists. You've discovered time in your schedule, and you have vowed not to waste it. You've even taken a look at how highly effective people bring these skills together to lead productive and happy lives.

And finally, you now know how to take out the nastiest monster of them all—procrastination. With procrastination out of your way, you have no further barriers to success. You will stop juggling and instead take your balancing act on the road. Remember:

Balance
Ultimately
Saves
You

I wish you the best of success in your future endeavors, and I hope to meet you along your journey, as your passion continues to take you on new and exciting paths to achieve goals you never thought possible.

For More Information . . .

For more information on how you can stop juggling, overcome procrastination, and get more done in less time, go to:

http://www.BusyBeingBusy.com or
http://www.MichellePrince.com.

Michelle Prince
"America's Productivity Coach"

The Ideal Professional Speaker for Your Next Event!

*Is Your Organization Busy Being Busy...
But Getting Nothing Done?*

"America's Productivity Coach," Michelle Prince, is on a Mission to Help Your Organization to Stop Juggling, Overcome Procrastination & Get More Done in Less Time in Business, Leadership & Life!

Michelle Prince knows a thing or two about being busy!

As a best-selling author, Zig Ziglar Motivational Speaker, business owner of multiple companies, wife of 15 years, and mother of two young boys, Michelle has learned the art of juggling her personal and professional life successfully. Most people are juggling too many things, procrastinating and not getting as much done as they want, which leads to a life of frustration and unfulfilled goals.

Michelle has learned the secret to living a happier, more abundant life, and she's on a mission to show orgainzations how to stop juggling, overcome procrastination, and get more done in less time in business, leadership, and life! It's time for "America's Productivity Coach," Michelle Prince, to give you the tools to STOP being busy *being* busy!

To schedule Michelle to Speak at Your Event:

469-443-8768

Info@PrincePerformance.com
http//www.MichellePrince.com

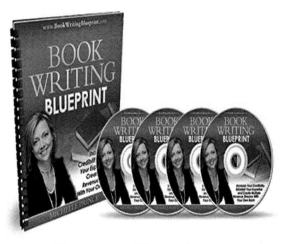

Procrastinating
on Writing a Book?

Take Michelle Prince's homestudy course: *Book Writing Blueprint*. In this course, you will learn how to increase your credibility, establish your expertise, and create multiple revenue streams with your own book.

You may not be sure you have any expertise to share, but you do! *Book Writing Blueprint* will guide you through the steps to deciding what to write about. It will also reveal 3 secrets for writing and publishing a book, as well as 5 easy steps to the writing process that ANYONE can follow.

You will have absolutely no excuse to procrastinate any longer, because Michelle Prince will take you every step of the way, from writing to editing to publishing and finally marketing your book.

Intrigued? Call 469-443-8768, visit http://www.BookWritingBlueprint.com, or email us at Info@PrincePerformance.com.

Would you like to be happier, more successful, have happier relationships, and live an extraordinary life?

Then, check out Michelle Prince's best-selling book *Winning in Life Now: How to Break Through to a Happier You!* In these pages, Michelle Prince will help you:

- Find your passion in life
- Believe that you have the power to achieve your goals
- Abolish negative self-talk that may be holding you back
- Embrace the uniqueness that is within you
- Overcome stress by balancing priorities in your life
- Banish worry
- Live each day as if it might be your last
- Motivate yourself to take action now

Order your copy today by calling 469-443-8768 or visiting http://www.WinningInLifeNow.com or emailing Info@PrincePerformance.com.